Ripple, Scar, and Story

Ripple, Scar, and Story

Poems by

Karla Huston

© 2022 Karla Huston. All rights reserved.
This material may not be reproduced in any form, published,
reprinted, recorded, performed, broadcast,
rewritten or redistributed without
the explicit permission of Karla Huston.
All such actions are strictly prohibited by law.

Cover design by Shay Culligan
Cover and author photo by Jennifer Selbrede Photography

ISBN: 978-1-63980-173-2

Kelsay Books
502 South 1040 East, A-119
American Fork, Utah 84003
Kelsaybooks.com

For Steven K. Huston, my love, my heart.
January 22, 1949–March 15, 2021

"i carry your heart (i carry it in my heart)" ee cummings

Much gratitude to those early and late readers of this book: Cathryn Cofell, DeWitt Clinton, Abayomi Animashaun, and Steve Polansky. Your input, your experience, and your encouragement are invaluable. Kisses to my daughters Rebecca Huston and Kimberly Huston for putting up with a poet mother who is likely to write about anything.

Acknowledgments

Grateful appreciation to the editors of following literary journals, anthologies, and websites where these poems were first published.

American Life in Poetry: "Lip"

Appleton Post Crescent: "A Theory of Frogs and Toads" Collaboration with Wm. Glasheen, video journalist

Blue Heron Review: "Theory of Numbness"

Bramble: "When My Father Had Gout"

Dandelion Farm Review: "History of Grit"

Doll Anthology: "Plie"

Double Kiss Anthology: "Where I Lived"

Request from Denise Sweet, past Wisconsin Poet Laureate, National Poetry Month. Facebook post: "A Fallen Sparrow"

Grief Bone: "First Memory," "Left Wrist"

International Crane Foundation: "Sandhill Cranes in the City"

One Art Poetry Journal: "Blame"

The Lake: "Descent"

Moss Piglet: "When Tennis Balls Were White," "Rolling Pin," "My Father, Drunk"

Rusty Truck: "Men at Work," "Ireland from 38,000 Feet," "Virtuoso in a Volvo"

Watermelon Isotope: "Ireland from 38,000 Feet," "Volcano"

Steam Ticket: "Resurrections"

Wisconsin Fellowship of Poets Calendar: "Moth Orchid"

Wisconsin People & Ideas: "Window Dressing"

Verse-Virtual: "At 79, My Father," "Moth Orchid," "Pancakes"

Waccamaw Review: "My Lips are Made of Wax, My Teeth are Furry Blades and Other Lies"

Contents

I

Where I Lived	15
History of Grit	16
Rolling Pin	17
Descent	18
Rag Rug	19
Weep Song	20
My Father's Horns	21
Lip	22
When My Father Had Gout	23
My Mother's Lost Teeth	24
When Tennis Balls Were White	25

II

Moth Orchid	29
Sandhill Cranes in the City	30
The Birds are Different Here	31
A Fallen Sparrow	32
A Theory of Frogs and Toads High Cliff State Park	33
Yellow Birch in April	35
Conger Road, Hayward, Wisconsin	36
Sportsmen's Bar	37
Men at Work	38
Lakes in Wisconsin	39
Early Mammoths of Los Angeles	40
In Consideration of Rocks	41
Ireland from 38,000 Feet	42

III

My Lips are Made of Wax, My Teeth are Furry Blades and Other Lies	45
Things I Ask My Toothbrush	46
Window Dressing	47
The Stone Owl Across the Street	48
At 79, My Father	49
Virtuoso in a Volvo	50
Tin Box	51
Plié	52
My Mother, Cutting My Bangs	53
First Memory	54
My Father, Drunk	55
Pancakes	56

IV

Counting	59
Blame	61
Queen of Broken Bones	62
French Twist	63
Left Wrist	64
Mannequins in Storage	65
Theory of Numbness	66
Blisters	67
Pine-Sol	68
The Cane	69
Resolutions	70

I

Where I Lived

The first thing you'll notice
is the cathedral of trees,
how branches reach, fold,
and hold up the light.
You might expect to see
a bride and groom pass under.
But not in this town.
The only thing brilliant
is a rattler swaying down Main
on a day so hot tomatoes wilt.
Around the corner—
the livestock auction hall—
cows wearing yellow earrings,
peer and swish up a ramp
where they're assessed
by farmers with straw teeth.
There are as many churches
as bars, a pool hall called The Hole
where boys come out smoking,
wearing girls with pointy bras.
That doorway is where a boy once
died for love, stabbing his heart
black with a sharpened pool stick.
His girl talked with a stick
in her mouth, its red end bobbing,
and she told the boy
she did not want her fire lit
by him or God or the damned
snake crawling up her skirt.

History of Grit

I used to eat sand—sand cakes, sand pies,
made in my sandbox, sandbakkels,
Norwegian cookies, not made from sand
but still gritty sweet. "She eats sand,"
my mother said to the neighbors
as I grinned, my cheeks stuck with it,
a few grains clinging to my lips. Sand
looked like brown sugar as I shoveled
with a cast-off spoon.

I loved sugar—on tomatoes, rice,
on cottage cheese. I loved the brown
sugar sandwiches I had for lunch
when the bologna ran out. I liked
the way it crunched between my teeth,
the buttery sweetness, the way it cooled
when it melted. I loved the way other kids
looked a little jealous.

Older, when I tried to impress boys,
I hated sand, the way it clung
to my baby-oiled shoulders
and itched as it filled the crevices
of my swimsuit. I'd shrug off the shawl
of it, wander to the water and let it wash me.
Later, there'd be sweetness.

Rolling Pin

This one came with ball bearings,
an easy spin about the world
of piecrusts and sugar cut-outs
as thin as Helga Lee's. It came
with warnings and snickers
about how a new wife might use it.
And why? No mention of cleavers
or fillet knives or a cast iron
skillet—all better substitutes
to cure behavior. New, mine
smelled like maple and promise.
Nearly 50 years later, the wood
is soft, its handles bent. It smells
of Crisco and butter, one crack
filled with flour, all of it
smooth as silk.

Descent

My father's mother was a shieldmaiden. Her hands
were mallets of fur and weft. She used them
to pound shuttles of rags through a loom.
Her rugs lay as still as sleeping children.

She wrapped warp around pins, hung cones
from spindles, counted piles of sewn rags, finger
to nose to finger: aught   aught.
The loom split and shuddered.

Grandmother's shield was her most righteous
armor. She hammered the Lord's Way. Her rugs
were legions of virtue and fringe. My
fingers were spools of yellow uncles.

Rag Rug

My grandmother wouldn't approve
of this one. All those slubs and loose threads.

Sloppy work, she'd say, carpet rags
not sewn right, end-to-end and not

on the bias. When ladies came
with bushel baskets of rolled rags,

she'd eye them once and know she'd need
to resew them before shoving shuttles

through her loom. It was the right way,
the only way she knew. And this rug

with its multicolored warp, also a no-no,
too showy for her German Lutheran taste,

where it was important to blend, become
invisible—the way most women did, then.

How she would've blushed today
with everybody showing their everything,

everywhere. This rug—all flash and bang,
lumps exposed, the slipshod selvage edge.

It's warm, though, when I step out of the shower,
catch the scent of her Cashmere Bouquet.

Weep Song

Pagan Goddess Brighid

You may think I'm a sweet
Gaelic girlie with red curls
and green eyes; don't be
confused. I am Minerva,
Athena and Brigit. I am
wisdom weaving, perpetual
music, echo of wells—
sacred and haunted. I tend
the flame, wail for what is lost,
mourning keen, weep song.
When you want someone to cry
for you, look for me. This
is a deep dirge, elegant trance—
for my son who died fighting.
What else can a mother do
but sob? I am waiting for snakes
to take me to him, my night
whistle calling the way.
I am fire arrow, one side of me—
beautiful, the other—
ugly and fierce. I wait
perpetually for spring.
I taught Banshees to sing.

My Father's Horns

Saturday nights he'd jam
the van: the upright
silver bass and the curly
sousaphone. Back then
the gang played standards, some
oom-pa-pas and little waltzes,
and packed the dance floor
with suits and circle skirts.
Sometimes a pretty woman sang.
My father drove home after,
half asleep, a little jazzed,
his throat choked with smoke.
The horns, their big bells silent,
settled once in the back.
Those Saturday night beauties—
the ones he held tight,
the ones he crooned to.
My mother—keeping
time at home.

Lip

When my father tuned his sousaphone,
he fiddled with tubes and oil

like when he restored the Model T, his hands
working the pipes and joints. And all around him

it's polka polka, big oom-pas, little dancing girls
on the tips of the valves while he worked his embouchure

into the proper purse of lips. Somewhere
bar lights glinted off the big bell, the name "Bob"

engraved inside the swale, hill and valley
little dancehall at the end of a corn maze,

small towns in Wisconsin, a fireman's dance
in a cavernous hall, a wedding gig or two.

He said nothing while he adjusted the weight
on knees already bruised and aching. When

cancer took a wedge out of his lip,
he had to give them up—The Beer Barrel,

the She's-Too-Fat, the Blue-Eyes-Cryin'-in-the-Rain
Polka, the Liechtensteiner, a schottische or two.

The music lived in his head, the tip of his tongue,
the records stacked and dusty on the floor.

When My Father Had Gout

My mother had asthma and anxiety,
high blood pressure and cholesterol,
sciatic pain and compression fractures
in her spine. My father had atrial
fibrillation and heart failure. He took
warfarin—rat poison—, he called it,
needing monthly blood tests, his arms
bruised like old peaches. On Sundays,
their kitchen table was a riot of pills
and containers and boxes labeled
by days. To my father's surprise,
my mother died of colon cancer.
He never quite believed the x-rays
but sent her death certificate
as proof of what he didn't want
to know. He took his pills, washed them
down with pizza, fried chicken,
bananas on the brink, those irradiated
meals and gin. When I suggested
he might eat better, he said he had
pills for that. The winter morning
I found him, his garage was filled
with hollow pizza boxes and pot-pies,
plastic clamshells, his pills boxes
empty on the kitchen table.

My Mother's Lost Teeth

She popped them out at whim,
my mother's false teeth—the shock
of seeing them on the end table
or the edge of the sink, a nightstand,
her upper lip sunk in rivulets
of wrinkles. She was buried in them,
I'm sure, so why did I find
this set in her bathroom closet?
Pink plastic gums—"gooms"
like brooms, she said—
and nearly white, a haze
of effervescence still clinging
to the surface. Now, around my neck,
a pendant made of her gold bridge,
replaced long ago with porcelain.
She'd tucked it into her wallet
waiting for me to find.

When Tennis Balls Were White

Back when tennis balls were white,
my father swatted lobs with my uncle.
I remember watching their long arms
reaching for the shot, the way their knees
bent and flexed into long volleys.
My father's legs burned, then tanned
in those days, his breath exploding
in his chest. That's what likely killed
him, years of smoke, and the solvent
he used to restore the old car, the Briscoe.
Back when tennis balls were white,
he took everything inside
where it stewed in the muck his lungs
would become, his heart missing
those tender parts, finally filled
with a fluid he could never quite expel
like a faulty spit valve
on the sousaphone he played
when tennis balls began to yellow.

II

Moth Orchid

This one was saved
from the sale table
at the garden center, a plant
I've nursed for two years,
and finally, the nose
of a shoot poked between
the broad paddles
of leaves, then a slender stem
with five small buds, winter-white
against a winter window,
and today's unwrapping
like a star, a small mouth
singing at its center.

Sandhill Cranes in the City

These two, a pair of thugs
looking for trouble, as we drove
by on a November morning.
They wore winter-gray coats,
backward red caps, their knobby
knees stiff in the cold. We stopped,
and wondered at them as they sorted
through a pile of corn. We stared;
they stared, shifting one leg
to another. They stepped closer,
perhaps curious about our car,
of the dog at the window who
was quickly at attention, ready
to help them on their way.
Then they ruffled their shoulders;
their song was not laughter but something
rolling with joy, daring them to lift
the earth with their wings.

The Birds are Different Here

Not the sweet chickadees
and raucous robins of Wisconsin,
no pairs of cardinals, brilliant
against snow and cold. The crows
are the same, though, coughing
their displeasure from high wires
and poles. I've heard

that when cardinals arrive,
They are a visit from the dead.
Here, there are riots of hummingbirds,
black peaked Phoebes, a few sparrows
and occasional bursts of parrots. No cardinals.
If you return, how will I know?

A Fallen Sparrow

Beak splat and feathers
on my window. It was windy
and bitter and I wore
thin pajamas, my hair still
wet from the shower.
I cupped him as his heartbeat
steadied. He ruffled his feathers
once. I held him until I, too, was cold,
then set him in a nest
of leaves and went inside.
This gray world wouldn't be
less for the loss of one sparrow,
but later, when spring leaves appear,
I might hear him singing,
a grateful song, perhaps,
and just for me.

A Theory of Frogs and Toads
High Cliff State Park

It might have begun with a kiss.
It might have begun with a frog
and a princess and a dare. It began
with a river of ice, a slow erosion,

a trickle of water between
dolostone and shale. It began
with miles of this: compression
and loosening and moving.

It began in this place, a pool near
a quarry and a road, with popple
and maple leaves wrinkling
and unfolding, a whisper in spring.

It might have begun with a kiss,
a love song, a cautious chirr, a whistle
or peep, a croak. It began in water.
Sperm floated over eggs, a drift and swell.

It ended in a pond like this, hidden
under a mantle of algae, under
the shadow of ash trees and rocks
where tadpoles waggled and swirled,

eventually losing their tails to become
what they would. It ended with frogs,
green and leopard and chorus,
and toads, plain or fancy or warted,

their backs cloaked in duckweed.
It ended in this place, under the shawl
of dark water, a frenzy of toads, of frogs.
When it began, you might have seen them.

You might have heard their choir of stories,
a promise only nature can keep,
their bulbous eyes watching just above
the surface in this place where it began,

frogs and toads singing their love. It began
with water and a river of ice,
a slow erosion. It began with a kiss.

Yellow Birch in April

It's fitting to find one outside this old
house, a retreat, a haven for writers,
where poets gather sharpened pencils
and stare out windows looking
for metaphors in spring's cruelties.
Its two trunks rise from one root
spread into the sky like gray smoke.
Branches reach above the roofline,
shiver with the wings of birds,
collect silvery pearls of rain.
Even without leaves, it is beautiful.
Once natives used the bark
of the yellow birch to dry and grind
into bread, the sap tapped to flavor
tea and medicines, the outer bark
used as skin for canoes. Writers
see only paper, the way the bark
curls and furls, the way their own
poor pages must look: wrinkled
and a bit desperate,
the only bright thing here—
the red cardinal, its beak split
with seed, flitting from idea to idea.

Conger Road, Hayward, Wisconsin

The spruce along the road
is clearly dead, no green
boughs to blend with others—
so many greens, it's impossible
to name them. Fiddlehead ferns, tall
popple with shaking leaves,
wide hearts of basswood. White
oaks waving, branches dipping,
ground cover teeming with green
and mosquitoes and tiny gnats.
This dead spruce, with its tarnished
needles glows like an orange torch.
Even in death there is beauty.
Each night loons mourn the loss;
The moon lights the lake with fire.

Sportsmen's Bar

There's one in nearly every small town
or along some two-lane
with owners named Smitty, Ole
or Hank. The bars have the same motif:
lighted beer signs in the windows—
they are always open—
a few pickups in the parking lot
if you could call it a lot. And around back,
a dumpster, pallets and empties—
cases and boxes, spent barrels.

Inside, a jukebox, shabby pool table,
maybe a few dusty mounts on the walls,
a Jackalope, a sorry-looking walleye.
There'll be racks of chips, Slim Jims
and lottery tickets along the back bar,
which is the best thing in the place,
polished with years of smoke
and solace, oaken with a mirror
so you can watch yourself tip a Pabst
or slug a shot of brandy. This bar is no

bistro or diner. If you want something
more than pickled pigs' feet or those
boiled eggs floating like eyeballs in brine,
you'll want to move along to the place
at the other end of town, the joint
where no one knows your name.

Men at Work

A passel of them, standing around
or operating heavy equipment,
hard-hatted and thick-booted,
while the machinery grinds
and growls, then backs up: beep
beepbeepbeep, circles and moves
forward. A wizard on a dozer picks up
buckets full of gravel or pushes
and moves, the excavator digs
or deposits debris, as delicate
as a woman setting plates and flatware
on white linen. Other men stop
to watch, hands in pockets, knees
locked or heels rocking, all of them
staring at the organized commotion.
The watchers, some of them with chairs
or walkers, memories of childhood
dirt piles, sand and yellow cast iron
caterpillars moving slowly
through their dreams, the dust clouds
and sifts. Everyone is touched by it.

Lakes in Wisconsin

Lakes have been pressed into the earth
by the rocky thumbs of glaciers,
the ice pulled back, leaving
its meltings behind, leaving kettles
and moraines and riots of rocks.
In Wisconsin, there are 59 lakes
named Long Lake, sometimes two
in a county. There are 82 named Bass
which might or might not be jumping
with them, and 116 named Mud.
In Wisconsin we boast that we have
more lakes than Minnesota
which claims 10,000. It all
depends on how you define a lake.
Wisconsin defines a lake as something
more than a finger's width deep—
like the lake of your bird bath,
the lake in your dog's water dish
or the deep wet pools of your eyes.

Early Mammoths of Los Angeles

Before stars were stars, before
they shined over the Hollywood sign
in Griffith Park, the biggest debuts
were Pleistocene mammoths
who stepped into the wide lake
of asphalt at the center of the city
before it became a city, the shore
a sticky, black chaos covered in dust
and leaves. Maybe mother mammoth
went looking for her calf who was stuck.
Then she became part of the mire.
Then saber tooth tigers took
advantage of their good fortune,
so many meals too easy to resist.
Dire wolves showed up to snack
on the tigers, and so the story goes,
the birth of a food chain, perhaps,
mammoth and tiger and wolf
howling misery into the dark night.
Today you can see them in their mucky glory,
smell their petrified breath—hear
the tangle of traffic near La Brea
and Wilshire in this the city of angels
and devils, the tar pits still a-bubble
waiting, like old stars, to be noticed again.

In Consideration of Rocks

Stop it already with the rocks.
Stop stacking them into precarious
cairns. Cease making bridges
in rivers and on shores. It's bad
for the ecosystem. Quit hauling
them home to line your driveway
and flower beds. That big one
on your lawn looks
odd next to the cowboy
silhouette. Quit skipping them across
smooth blue lakes; they sink. Quit
making pets out of them, naming
them Bubba or Betty. Stop the endless
tumbling, canisters filled with smaller rocks,
the grinding that can smooth the edges
of a rasp. Please stop painting them
to look like cacti or ladybugs
or hedgehogs. No homilies
or affirmations, either, no pleas to deities.
No one needs to see that.

Ireland from 38,000 Feet

Not exactly a patchwork, not
exactly a paisley print.
Small pieces of earth, woods,
rivers connected with stone
fences and puffs of green,
flags of wheat, spikes of corn,
those of flowering tiny rooftops.
I imagine a land of mischief
and banshees and love poems.
Dark rooms of monks scribbling
their poor verses in the margins
of fields. Somewhere below
a man drinks his sorrows,
a woman worries hers, children
shriek and splash, the gods of long ago
swirl through their dreams.
We are traveling too fast. I can't
hear the green stones calling,
only crying babies, a shift
of sky as we move through it,
the sizzle and whine in my ears:
you're almost there.
You're almost there.

III

My Lips are Made of Wax, My Teeth are Furry Blades and Other Lies

My hair is a bristly statue. My ears
are gramophones; a small dog sits
on my shoulder and cries into them.

My nose is a funnel of love. My lips
are made of wax, sweet and red and chewy.
My teeth are furry blades, chipped and rusty.

My neck is a chicken wattle, a ratchety
bobble and swing and sway.
I'm looking out for an axe.

I am always the brave one,
never fearing fathers, husbands,
brothers, and other small gods.

My throat is conch shell, listen
to the city in it, the swoosh and hush;
my breasts are a trio of ringing bells.

My arms are not wings, nor a flight of angels,
nor—. My fingers are mechanical
pawls—my thumbs, blunt sockets.

My fingers are quills scratching words.
My belly is an inkwell—hips are two trains
running headlong into the dry gulch of my belly.

My knees are knocking, but no one can come in.
My feet are ready to answer
but they don't know the secret word.

Things I Ask My Toothbrush

Are you listening, instead,
of standing in the corner
like a post, waiting for me
to pick you up, add a squirt
of something minty and turn you
on? Forgive me for not holding
you more, for not wrapping
my fingers around your sleek buzz
filling my hand more than twice a day.
Some days I've eaten
my body weight in Gouda
or buttercream, teeth furry,
tongue gone to putty.
Then I need you, want you
to cut through the muck.
Toothbrush, how you make me
shine, mouth shivering
teeth slick and cool
and white as Chiclets.

Window Dressing

The woman in the window
banged off plastic arms, twisting
the waist loose, then shimmied silk
dresses over hard shoulders and hips.
She loved heads the best, the way
she could remove the skull cap,
reach in to adjust the backs
of the eyes, then face them where they
needed to look. In spring, she'd strew
silk tulips, gardenias and leaves
linking them together. Outside,
shoppers stopped to peer through slits
in the gray muslin and vowed to return.
Inside the resin women stared
into the wall of glass, that vacant
wishful look. Were they expecting
the men from the opposite window
to save them, their chiseled chins
glowing like lighthouses? The children
at their feet with their baskets
and bonnets, their bright Mary Janes,
wondered, long after the curtain fell,
if anyone would notice them, see
how their hunger lingered long
after the light spilled
into the street below them.

The Stone Owl Across the Street

Perched on a plinth of concrete,
it's been waiting in the same spot
for years, gray owl, rooted and silent,
its tail only anticipating flight, perhaps
a low, slow ascent over piney bushes
where mice huddle and squeak
about possible bits of seed, a last
meal, perhaps, before the coming
ice and snow. The owl will wait
there forever if we let him.

At 79, My Father

got pulled over by a county cop
for speeding on Highway M,
his MINI Cooper a streak of light
on those country roads.
Oh, Dad, what were you thinking?
as I sorted through countless
saved pages and found the warning ticket.
Myriad stacks ran the path from
his office, creating tunnels between them.

As a teen he worked gathering rocks
to clear a railroad tunnel.
He said the scariest part
was getting out of the way
of the train—there was no room—
as it rumbled through, him
jumping to the side, the grumble
of the engine, the searching
yellow light from the loud
stone walls to warn him.

Virtuoso in a Volvo

An excavator, not a car,
the kind that can flatten a house
in three swipes, then spin on its track
and pluck cut limbs and lay them
gently in a truck bed. This one's a noisy
thug while the engine warms in front
of my house, roadwork the order of the day.
The operator is wearing Day-Glo
yellow, a shirt with cut off sleeves. He's
bellied and bearded, jeans slung low,
his hair wispy as wheat in a breeze.
But behind the levers of this machine,
he is a genius of concrete and wet clay.
Deep below the street, the bucket digs
and with a flick of a steel wrist,
picks up a load, positions its burden of muck
and tips it gently into a waiting receptacle.
How delicate this dance, such power
and precision; I can't help but admire him
and marvel at his training,
his instincts and sense of balance.
My house shudders at the thought,
then settles for more.

Tin Box

Today, filled with my fountain pens,
the box looks like it belongs to me.
I'd seen it many times before
but rarely was allowed to open it—
the old chocolates box kept
in my parents' dresser with its
hinged top, its fancy butterflies
and pastoral vignette of swans
and failing light. It once stored orphan
keys and spent batteries and one
small magnifying glass. The keys
are still homeless, the batteries still
of no use. But the magnifying glass,
its cloudy eye, dusted with age,
can sometimes see into the past,
the pens—you know
what to do with pens.

Plié

My aunt's bedroom was a place
I was rarely allowed
with its lace and bows, dancers
embroidered on pillow cases,
the doll on the bed, crocheted
ruffles spilling from her waist.
Even the dressing table,
fancy and curved, the candy pink
skirt delicate and sweet.
The girl under the silver dome
always on her toes,
arms circled, pink tutu rippling,
as she twirled to *"Für Elise."*
I wanted to touch her
fingers, so delicate, they might
break. There was no touching
at my grandmother's house
and every time I asked, my aunt
covered the music box while the girl
bowed and folded inside herself.

My Mother, Cutting My Bangs

She steadied her hand as I sat
before her, perched on the edge
of the kitchen counter. My head
had been crammed under a faucet, a rag
held over my eyes to keep the soap
out while she sudsed, shampooed, rinsed
with the aluminum tumbler nearby.
I was rubbed and toweled, my bangs
flattened, Scotch-taped against my brow.
She came at me with scissors, sharp
as my grandmother's tongue, while she
snipped, snipped—swore, but my bangs
wouldn't comply and stay even.
They shrank from the shears, backing
away, getting shorter but no less
straight. She stepped back, sighed,
her work done for that day, at least.
My bangs, crooked and unruly
became an abstract painting against
the pale canvas of my forehead
a glimmer of the scissors-wielding
woman I, too, would someday become.

First Memory

My mother clinking plates in the sink.
My father sits in the big chair,
sifting through news, the crackle
of the paper as he straightens
pages, the click-whoosh of his Zippo,
the sizzle of the cigarette
as it catches fire, smoke drifting
like vines, nearby, the lamp a floating
cone of light, me floating behind it
to see where the cord led, small fingers
finding the open outlet. Then
my father rising, papers falling,
my mother rushing, calling. She said
it happened. I could not
have remembered; I was only two.
Yet, I can still see the way the light
seemed to pull the roses and ivy
from the walls. I remember the shock.
The way they bolted toward me.
I don't remember that, only
the shadows that pulled me, memory
drifting like smoke. Both gone,
now, the moment is mine alone,
a show of slides to arrange
when I need to see them, the frames
shuffling to capture the time
when it happened—or didn't.

My Father, Drunk

My aunt complained as he down-shifted
around the corner and roared
past her house late at night
after beers at Krome's bar. In letters
to his girlfriend (my mother),
while away at school, he fessed up
to swearing off whiskey and beer.
Older while playing dance jobs,
he'd nurse a whiskey soda
for hours. After my mother
died, I taught him to drink gin
from green bottles, tonic begging
to go flat after the third one.
Still, he rarely slurred his words
even as he showed me all the old photos,
the two of them woozy
from rides at the county fair.
So young, so dizzy
with first love.

Pancakes

Those almost round beauties,
those stacks of happiness
that seemed to hover on the plate.
They're weighted by sunny pats
of butter and syrup,
maple—if you're lucky—
liquid sugar puddled
and dispersed, drizzled
into pools, pancakes
like small rafts
floating in the blueberry
lake of your plate.

IV

Counting

> "We counted everything" Hayden Saunier
> —from *How to Wear This Body*

I count everything, too, including steps—
at my house, six down, another six down.
Then up. Some stairways are so narrow
and worn, I can count those steps by half.

I used to count the seconds my dog
peed, either squatting or leg lifted
on my rose bush. I started when he
was a pup-in-training, hoping he'd
empty his bladder to last all night.

As a kid, I counted gifts under the tree,
the blocks from school to home, how many
times my brother knuckle-punched my thigh.
I counted daisy petals over and over
until they equaled "he loves me."

I wonder, now, as I count syllables
in a line, lines in a poem, numbers
ticking in my head,
like the metronome my grandfather used
to measure his music, perhaps
counting is a meditation, a way
to control what I can't—or won't.

Mostly, I count steps—up, down,
until it becomes habit like breathing.
I count them in the dark, me at the top
step, dog peeing in the snow, minus 15
and no moon. "Hurry," I say,

one-two-three times until I realize
he won't come till he's ready,
that counting is what our
heart does—until it breaks.

Blame

The only thing I ever stole
was a tube of lipstick from K-Mart.
All my friends were doing it—so
easy, they said. And there it was—
in my pocket, little flame
of a crime, burning next to
the dollar I could've used
to pay for it, the money I was
saving to buy the new Beatles 45.
The lipstick grew hot in my pocket.
When I got home and tried it,
the color turned greasy on my lips,
a greenish shade of guilt.
My lips were thick with it.
So I wrapped the tube in tissue
and buried it deep in the trash
my father would soon burn.
Every time I stirred the ash:
little glints of melted
plastic and gold, a color
that never looked good on me.

Queen of Broken Bones

At last count: three ankle breaks,
same ankle. Left wrist requiring
surgery, metal and screws. Ribs
broken as a result of the wrist,
frozen shoulder—same cause.
More broken ribs as a result
of an over-zealous chiropractor.
Kneecap buckle: two surgeries.
Sprains and pulled muscles from
coughing or tripping or falling.
Maybe it's my ears—a family
trait, big with floppy lobes
that continue to grow—
cartilage, they say. Maybe
it's a balance problem—
also related to ears.
I'm careful, take calcium,
hold onto handrails, walk only
lighted pathways. I wonder how
I've made it this far.

French Twist

I've tried most of my life to perfect it,
except sixth grade when I had
a pixie cut. I'd comb my hair
with my fingers, quick twirl and tuck.
Grace Kelly wore a French twist, so did
Kim Novak in *Vertigo*.
When I worked at a golf pro shop,
I wore my hair in a bun—my ponytail ratted
and smoothed over a bristle roller
and pinned. Perfect for my waitress job.
I wore a hairnet. Don asked me
for a date where he grabbed my hand
as he led me to the dance floor.
He closed his eyes and bit his lip
as we swayed to the music.
He had only one request—
that I wear my hair long. I may have
been blonde, but I wasn't Grace Kelly.
Too many pimples, not enough
Hollywood for the perfect twist and tuck.

Left Wrist

Good-bye, dear wrist, small runway
to my hand—the way you flex
and extend, how I love your soft
blonde hairs, the way you shrug
into my sleeve when I'm cold.
Good-bye to the underside, skin
pale as milk, a blue river of blood pulsing
through, sweet freckle and lump.
Today you are broken, skin purpled
and swollen, but tomorrow, you
will be cut and probed, bones poked
into place, then plated and screwed
into something stronger, better,
perhaps bionic. So long to the old.
Goodbye to the smooth
and pristine. Hello ripple,
scar and story.

Mannequins in Storage

They stare from where they are left,
each standing on a chrome pole,
leaning on each other for balance

on the tilting wooden floor.
When no one is around,
they gather broken arms

and chipped fingers, try to assemble
better versions of themselves
so whenever the freight elevator

drags its chains and begins
its slow pull or the moon outside
lowers itself for a long look,

the mannequins stop their collecting.
Some, with hips cocked left, some right,
some with toes pointing backwards,

one with its lone arm reaching.
All of them with hard lips pursed, eyes
looking everywhere at once.

Theory of Numbness

After a trip to the dentist,
the left side of my face sagged
like an old pair of socks;
even smiling hurt. Finally,
my old face lifted and returned.
Yet days later, my cheek still tingled,
the bruise of the deed
under cover of flesh and muscle.
If you ignore it, pain sometimes
goes away, but another ache
takes its place, the ghost of it
frozen in you, so deep—the shadow
of something you don't know you
need till you see that it's gone.

Blisters

Pockets of fluid trapped by friction
like new shoes that ride up your heels
or the ones across a thumb from raking
without gloves. Blisters of tar, the way
they bubbled between cracks in the street.
Even though your mother told you
not to, you popped them with bare toes.
Or bubble-packs of pills. Impossible
to open with thumbs or teeth.
Everything packed that way to prevent
theft even after you've paid for it. Cold
sores that begin with a tickle
and end in a canker that cracks
when you smile. Or the blister of ink
in a cartridge, the bubble of ink on the tip
of your pen. Your shoulders, nose
after too much sun. You peel in sheets
and layers. A chef who picks up
a searing hot spoon, raises welts
on her fingertips. Still, she cooks.
The girl in the dive bar kitchen
who backed up and put her hand
into the fryer, her blisters
turned to scars, became reminders
of everything that continued to hurt.

Pine-Sol

I learned to clean from the best:
my mom and her moist
finger, my grandmother with her
Electrolux, watching them beat
rugs on the line, lace curtains
stretched and gathering sun. It felt good,
after finishing in my chores, to know
most of the detritus was binned—
except for those birch seeds which look
like tiny *fleur de lis* still stuck
in the rug and resistant
to my licked finger.

The Cane

When my grandmother broke
her kneecap, I didn't see it happen
but heard about it in those hushed
tones parents used when they didn't
want kids to know the gory
details. I heard "tripped" and "fell"
on the sidewalk, and I imagined
cracked and heaving cement squares.
I heard "hospital" and knew this
was serious business. They said that
she was coming to our house, a half
block away, through her back yard,
past the roses and garden
into the cinder alley. Had she brought
a pint of raspberries or plate
of Plough Tucker? Did she wear
her good apron with the smocked pockets?
Gardening shoes and wide hat?
My grandmother was a strong woman.
She mended well and wove rugs
and tended violets and peonies.
Her only scar was the letter C
branded into her kneecap. I didn't
know what a kneecap was then. I only
knew she'd be limping for a while.
This bamboo cane with its carved
circles on the handle, must have been hers.
It's shorter than my grandfather's,
just right for her and maybe someday, me.

Resolutions

Promises to yourself don't count.
You cannot be trusted not
to change your mind. Walk slowly
on ice. Rubber shoes with or without
tread won't help. If you fall, you'll hit
your ass first, then back, then head.
This will hurt a lot
and feeling sorry for yourself
won't make it better. Steer clear
of frozen dog turds or the man
who laughs, then looks quickly
to see who's watching. He'll tease
you until tickling hurts, then touch
your skin with a just-snuffed match
to see if fire will burn twice.
Being yourself will never be good
enough for some people. Don't talk
when no one is listening. Your better
angel would tell you this is bullshit.
Let your pen do the talking.

About the Author

Wisconsin Poet Laureate 2017–2018, Karla Huston was a life-long resident of Wisconsin until her move to Southern California in 2020. Her poetry finds its roots in the stories we tell, those memories which define us as human. As Poet Laureate, she nurtured poetry among the elderly and memory-impaired by working with Memory Cafés.

Huston speaks regularly at book festivals, writing conferences about the public value of poetry and the arts. She taught poetry writing workshops at The Mill: A Place for Writers in Appleton for ten years and served on the board of directors for The Mill: A Place for Writers, Council for Wisconsin Writers, and the Fox Valley Writing Project.

The author of eight chapbooks of poems, Huston received an Outstanding Achievement Award from the Wisconsin Library Association for her full collection, *A Theory of Lipstick* and her chapbook *Grief Bone.* Huston's work has garnered many writing awards, including a Pushcart Prize for the poem "Theory of Lipstick" in 2012. Her writing has earned her residencies at the Ragdale Foundation, the Bread Loaf Writers' Conference, Write On, Door County and Shake Rag Alley.

www.ingramcontent.com/pod-product-compliance
Lightning Source LLC
Chambersburg PA
CBHW031204160426
43193CB00008B/499